THE RIGHT IS MASCULINE, THE LEFT IS FEMININE, LIBERTARIAN IS NON-BINARY: AN ESSAY ON GENDER AND POLITICS

Russell Hasan

CONTENTS

INTRODUCTION

This essay is a chapter from my much larger book, "To Be Loved, Love; To Be Liked, Be Nice to People; To Be an Adult, Forgive People: Emotions and Social Interactions, Explained." This is the chapter that explains gender, and then explains politics by reference to the idea that the political Right is masculine and the political Left is feminine, and the political expression of non-binary is Libertarian (Social Left plus Economic Right), in terms of the expression of gender-roles in politics.

It's an important analysis, which I felt deserved to be abstracted out and published as a standalone essay. This makes the material shorter, more focused, and easier to read.

DEFINITIONS:
+N, –N

To: at, directed at, towards.

For: Because of the morality and moral debts or moral credits of, for the benefit of.

+: Plus.

–: Minus.

N: An amount, a quantity.

As: Manifested as, embodied as, taking the form of.

$: Physical.

+N: Positive energy

Being there, showing up, staying, not leaving

Emotional support

Love

Happiness

Pleasure

Kindness

Hope

Trust

Compassion

Politeness

Respect

Friendliness/Being Friendly

Cheerfulness/Good Cheer

Optimism

Commitment

Honesty/Openness

Emotional availability

Doing work to make a relationship work

Appreciation

Being supportive in the face of negativity

Staying positive

Giving them a loan of social or emotional capital

–N: Negative energy

Not showing up/Leaving early

Rejecting someone

Keeping someone waiting/Sending someone away

Pain

Anger

Sorrow

Misery

Distrust

Pessimism

Gloom

Hopelessness

Depression

Sadness

Guilt

Shame

Rudeness

Disrespect

Theft of emotional capital

Negativity

Being annoying

Being manipulative

Being insecure (to lack trust)

Being emotionally dysfunctional

Being abusive

+$N:
Logistical support
Money
Tangible achievement
Tangible favors
Being relied upon
Doing work
Making stuff
Physical love

−$N:
Theft of money
Dishonesty
Being unreliable
Being manipulative
Using someone as a means to an end
Taking stuff
Physical violence

Y: The Self, You.

O: The Other, another person.

G: A Goal, any goal, any end state that is the object of desire.

MEN AND WOMEN

Definitions:

G: Any Goal, any end result or goal or objective that a person seeks or desires to obtain. Any goal that Y or O pursue.

Anger, aggression, force:

Y seeks Goal G from O by Y –N to O Exceeds O –N to Y.

The primary quality for causing –N is strength, to cause –N to O, and toughness to withstand pain, to accept –N from O without yielding to O. These are often thought of as a man's virtues. As such, the path of aggression and force is often associated with masculinity.

Attractiveness, pleasantness, trade:

Y seeks Goal G from O by O +N to Y as G for Y +N to O.

The primary qualities for causing +N are attractiveness, beauty, social skills, and emotional IQ. These are often thought of as a woman's virtues. As such, the path of attractiveness and beauty is often associated with femininity.

Trade, in economics, is often considered masculine, but peacefulness is seen as feminine, and trade is the inherently peaceful way to seek G, in contrast to force, which is the inherently warlike or argumentative way to seek G.

The paradigmatic relationship of man to woman is Woman +N to Man for Man –N to Enemies where Man's –N to Enemies Exceeds Enemies –N to Woman. The man uses aggression and strength to protect the woman from their enemies, and the woman is nice to the man in return and gives beauty and pleasantness to the man in return.

This is the model of gender that existed for cavemen in the last Ice Age, and during the Dark Ages and ancient times. The prototypical, paradigmatic caveman model is that:

the man hunts for food, by hunting animals, (aggression)

and he fights other men, if they threaten or approach the woman, (toughness)

and he fends off predators, by fighting off wild

animals, (strength)

while, in return,

the woman gives the man sex, (beauty, attractiveness)

and she raises the children, (social skills and emotional IQ)

and the woman gives emotional support to the man (social skills and emotional IQ)

and she keeps the man happy. (pleasantness)

So the man needs strength and aggression and toughness, and the woman needs beauty, social skills, and being emotionally adept.

The mathematical formula: Woman +N to Man for Man −N to Enemies.

Woman loves man, and her love forms their family, and, in return, man protects woman from their shared common enemies, man protects woman from danger, and man fights battles for woman.

Women would express their emotions, as +N to Man or as Woman's Need for +N from Man, but a man would not express his emotions, because this would be perceived as a sign of weakness, as Man −N to Man as Getting Emotional and being Vulnerable for Man +N to Man as being Emotionally sensitive and Managing his Emotions. Any sign of −N to Man would be interpreted as a sign of weakness, that would lessen the degree to which Man –N to Enemies Exceeds Enemies –N to Man. So women are thought of as emotional, while men are thought of as tough. Women always tell men to ask for help, but a man never wants to be helped in order to do something, because needing help is a sign of weakness, and a man always wants to be strong.

However, in modern times, anyone: man, woman, or any person, of any gender, can choose to use +N as a tool to achieve Goal G, or could choose to wield –N as a tool for seeking Goal G. They are not inherently limited to either gender, at least not in today's world. +N is the path of peaceful trade of value for value, of getting what you want by being good-looking and attractive and being nice and polite to people. –N is the path of getting into a fight in order to win and to conquer.

In traditional times, men used muscle to defeat their enemies. In modern times, a new type of man has emerged: the masculine nerd geek, who uses his brainy intelligence and his high IQ, instead of his muscles, to cause –N to his enemies, such as, for example, by devising schemes and plans to cause pain to his enemies, or by using his intelligence to figure out a way to defeat his enemies. A businessperson or lawyer, for example, wins in business, or in court, not by punching his enemy in the face and beating them up, but by outsmarting them, by making sales and crafting advertising campaigns, or by filing the correct motions and persuading a judge. The businessperson's success comes at the expense of his direct competitors, just as the lawyer's victory comes at the expense of his trial adversary, so those are fights, but fought with IQ, not with muscle.

In today's world, the attribute of causing –N to others has also served men well in business, and in sports, both of which can be viewed as competitions where you win by inflicting more –N onto your opponents than the amount of –N they inflicted onto you, such that If Y –N to O Exceeds O –N to Y, Then Y wins. It is a contest where the size of –N matters, and the biggest –N wins.

This may explain why business, and sports, are often male-dominated. A woman could succeed, in business, or in sports, but, to enjoy great success, she would have to win by inflicting –N onto her enemies, not by exceeding others' +N with her +N. Because that is how you win in a fight. And professional sports, and competition in free market capitalist business, are, ultimately, types of fights. You fight the other team to score more points. Or you fight the other competing businesses in your market for market share.

This book explains ways to defuse fights by means of projecting +N and Forgiveness of –N, but that doesn't "win the fight," it instead causes the two people to not have a fight. The focus of this book is on social skills, and using +N to achieve Goals, so the strategy and tactics to win by means of –N are not discussed in this book. But a person has to understand the +N and –N psychological dynamics, in order to read how people are behaving in a social situation, whether someone is trying to use +N, or whether someone is looking to have a fight and wield –N. There are situations where +N can defeat –N if the size of the +N Exceeds the size of the –N directed against it. The light of your positive energy outshines the darkness of their evil. However, if you face someone using negativity to achieve their goals, and if your +N does not Exceed their –N, if they are more negative than you are positive about whatever is involved, and if you are not willing to actually have a fight and have your –N Exceed their –N by being more mean and rude and angry and cruel and nasty and abusive and insulting than they are, then the other option is to walk away from that situation. Those are the three choices you have, most of the time: use +N, use –N, or walk away. Your approach should be that you should read the situation, and then choose the best option from among those three choices to achieve your Goals.

Insecurity about being a man or being

a woman, and how this can be exploited psychologically for manipulation, is discussed elsewhere in this book.

Definitions:

Aggression: The willingness to seek out and engage in risks and dangers without fear, under the belief that you can cause an –N that exceeds the –N that can be done to you.

Strength: The ability to cause –N to Enemies. For example, being able to craft mean, hurtful insults and formulate verbal abuse.

Toughness: The ability to withstand –N that Enemies cause to You, without crumbling or giving in or being defeated. For example, the ability to be verbally insulted in a brutal, hurtful way, without really caring about it and without feeling pain or suffering from it.

Assertiveness: the quality of trying to take control of any situation you are in, and to assert yourself and assert your beliefs and goals and desires onto any situation.

Attractiveness: The ability to give +N to the Other. For example, beauty as a set of sensations that cause pleasure.

Social IQ: The ability to manage a trade of +N for +N, or of +N to O for O –N to Enemies. The ability to manage emotions and expectations in a long-term relationship, for example.

Positivity: The ability to cause +N in general, to both Self and Others. Being nice, for example.

"The men fight while the women flirt." Or, to quote the rock band Garbage, "The boys wanna fight while the girls just want to dance all night." Given the textbook caveman gender roles of Woman +N to Man for Man –N to Enemies (man fights other men, fights predators, hunts food, for woman), we can see that, in the traditional gender roles social and social psychological dynamic, Assertiveness and Aggression and Toughness and Strength are Masculine virtues, for Men, because they are used to win a fight, while attractiveness, social IQ, and positivity, are Feminine virtues, for Women, because these are what Women need to survive and trade in return by getting the Men to protect them and fight their battles for them.

Obviously, in Third Millennium Earth, with our modern contemporary progressive views on gender, this traditional caveman view of gender is laughable and absurd. But, still, the role of Man and the role of Woman in this social dynamic does still explain a great deal about the actual behavior of men and women in real life. Whenever the size of – N to challenged, whenever a man's –N is challenged, he will fight back, and resist, against any perceived force that seeks to demean his manhood. Women tend to become insecure in, and can be goaded into compensating for, their ability to give +N, for example insecurity about their beauty, or fear of a failure in social skills, such as not being popular.

But "man" and "woman," in this sense, are gender roles that any human person can perform, such as, for example, women in women's sports causing –N to the other team in a fight to win a game, or women in business using their high IQ to cause –N to win economic wars against competing businesses in their marketplaces, are women winning in a man's fight, or men in fashion and beauty industries being good at causing +N, or men as actors in the theater or movies known for their good looks, are men succeeding in a woman's industry. But you would tend to see men who perform the male gender role to gravitate towards and be more interested in areas where –N causes success, like sports (strength to cause –N) or business and technology (where high IQ is used to cause –N to opponents), and women who perform the female gender role as more interested in areas where attractiveness leads to success, like getting married and raising a family or child education (where teaching social IQ to children causes success) or customer service or fashion or music or internet/ social media (where producing +N for an audience causes success).

In politics, the Right tends to be the more Manly, Masculine side. The Right value strength, and assertiveness, and domination against enemies (in foreign policy and wars, for example), and they view government control and regulations as a challenge to their manhood as the king of their household and independent ruler of their own life, and they value the toughness to be resilient against pain and to take a beating without getting knocked down.

In contrast, the Left tends to be more on the Womanly, Female side. The Left wants everyone to be taken care of and that no one should ever have to take risks or face danger, and everyone must always be protected by someone else (by the government), and they want everyone to always be treated in a nice respectful way, with people not being allowed to ever be mean or rude or disrespectful.

Socialism is, in essence, the forced feminization of the populace, placing the populace into a role of female weakness and helplessness to then be protected by the government in the role of male. As such, the men of the Right bristle at, and reject, all socialism, while socialism is cheered by the women and LGBTQs of the Left, and by the men of the Left who feel destined to assume the role of government with its power and authority to protect those women and LGBTQs on their behalf. Any group whose identity and sense of self-esteem comes from being a victim and from projecting self-pity and needing to be protected by someone else, would also naturally fall into the female position of weakness in relation to a male government as protector, and they would naturally support socialism. (The math for self-pity is Y −N to O for

Y as Self-Pity, where Y perceives that O owes +N to Y as sympathy but O isn't giving +N to Y to Y's satisfaction. It is similar to other such psychological dynamics, such as loneliness and/or depression as Y –N to O for O owes +N to Y as comfort, or Y –N to O as grouchy moodiness for O owes +N to Y as cheering up.)

Socialism imposes womanhood onto the public, and the socialist government claims the man's role as protector, and so the men of the Right inherently feel that socialism challenges their manhood as individuals and seeks to deny and take away their status as men, which would make them feel weak in relation to their own women and feel unable to fight their battles as men. So the Right will always oppose any position that the Left takes, for government and regulations and policy, and they will oppose them for the sake of opposing them, for the sake of preserving their masculinity, and not because they have a substantive rational objection to why this or that policy will not work, even if, by random chance, the government's position is objectively correct, and opposition is crazy, for that particular political issue. This explains why the Right sometimes takes positions that are crazy: they do so in order to oppose the Left, not because they really care about the issue itself. The Right would favor personal responsibility and, for example, gun ownership or the freedom to run a business, because the men of the Right feel competent to fight their battles themselves, and to win, instead of needing the government to fight their battles for them.

While the Left claims to be progressive on gender, the Left's political gender dynamic is, ultimately, merely a variation of the traditional caveman psychological dynamic, where the caveman government protects the cavewoman public and fights all battles on her behalf.

The Fascism of the Right, is, in essence, the forced masculinization of a society, where an entire nation is put into a state of masculine anger and aggression, and the goal is to dominate all enemies and triumph by conquest. The fascists' goal is to win all fights by means of their –N exceeding the enemy's –N, so they want to be as negative as possible, and their strategy is to engage in any and every fight possible, for this purpose: to strengthen their powers of –N to be as high as possible, because every fight that they win tests, hones, and improves their powers of causing –N. Fascists tend to persecute political dissidents and to punish dissent as Y –N to O, and they also tend to seek out wars of conquest as Y –N to O, as fighting for the sake of fighting, conflict solely for the purpose of making a display of manly, muscular strength. They have no mercy and no sympathy, and they walk the path which, in history, belonged to, for example, the Roman soldier or the Viking warrior, as bloodthirsty conqueror.

In contrast to socialism and fascism, in a libertarian, liberal, free democracy, such as today's

United States of America, each individual has the liberty to choose his, her, or their, gender role for themselves, and there is no national gender imposed upon society.

The Right tends to want men in male gender roles and women in female gender roles, because their men and women still rely upon "men being men" in the caveman model, their men need to be men, and their women rely on their men to be men for them, so they become insecure about their gender roles when they face gender-fluidity and their gender is challenged. That explains their love of tradition, it dates back to the caveman dynamic, which, to be fair to the Right, is how humans evolved 10,000 years ago and how we survived until the past century.

The Left is more gender-fluid and LGBTQ, which defines them as more progressive and modern, because they are more willing to have anyone in any gender role, and they can use women in male roles or men in female roles with success, and so they are less dependent upon men acting out the male gender role in order for their men and women to survive.

Despite the fact that strength and power are Right virtues and softness and sensitivity are Left virtues, Right and Left do not necessarily correlate to Right control/dictatorship and Left freedom/ democracy, it is not true that the Right is always dictatorial and the Left is always pro-freedom. Each could be either. The freedom Right are, for example, the libertarians. The dictatorial/control Right are the fascists, who desire total control by a dictator. The dictatorial/control Left are the socialists, the communists, and the progressives, who desire total control by the government. The democracy/freedom Left would be, for example, moderate center-left tax-and-spend liberals. Tyranny is the condition of total control, regardless of whether it is by a Right dictator or by a Left government. In contrast, true freedom requires democracy and civil liberties and a free press, regardless of whether the Left or the Right is the political party that happened to most recently obtain the most votes.

Economic freedom tends to be male freedom, the freedom for the strong: free market capitalism, gun rights, no government control. Social freedom tends to be female freedom, the freedom to be beautiful, or freedom for the weak: things being being nice and polite and being free from rudeness and from offensive behavior, abortion rights, LGBTQ rights, gay marriage, or, as a type of freedom to be weak, protection from racism, the right to use recreational hard drugs, immigration freedoms.

The social Right tends to be, not freedom, but men attacking female freedom, and men oppressing women: preventing women from having abortions, attacking the legal rights of transgender female youth, attacking the freedom to engage in LGBTQ sex or LGBTQ identity, etc. Similarly, the economic

Left tends to be, not freedom, but men attacking male freedom on behalf of women, and men oppressing other men, such as men telling other men what they have to do, how they have to behave, forcing people to conform to safety instead of taking risks, and forcing them to obey the government, instead of just letting them do whatever they want.

The Right is masculine, the Left is feminine, and Libertarian is the political non-binary, Libertarians are on the Right on economics and on the Left on social issues.

Envision a grid, where the Right side is male, the Left side is female, the bottom is Collective, and the top is Individual.

Right: Masculine: Collectivist - Fascists, Social Conservatives: Men rule men and women on behalf of men, domination, 100% controlled by men, women are oppressed, (often) a dictator, but economic freedom because that gives men the freedom to use their strength and intelligence, and freedom such as gun rights because that gives men the freedom to engage in physical violence, and freedom to be rude or offensive.

Left: Feminine: Collectivist - Socialism, the Economic Left: Men rule men and women on behalf of women in order to protect women, 100% controlled by men for women, no economic freedom, but (often) social freedom for women's rights, such as freedom from the rude and offensive, freedom for abortion, LGBTQ freedom, etc. There is an emphasis on safety, that the government will protect everyone (weak women) so that no one has to be strong enough to win a fight (as a man), and also the government will force everyone to be nice, polite, and respectful, so that there will be only female beauty, and no male ugliness, that is visible in discourse. They also champion the ideal of equality on the belief that men ruling for women will bring the women up to equal status as men, that the weak and oppressed will be lifted up to the level of the ruling class, by a ruling class that fights for the rights of the weak.

Right: Masculine: Individualist - Far Right Libertarians (Market Anarchists, Anarcho-Capitalists): There is no government, only market anarchy, so there is 100% freedom for men, because there is no government to nag them and whine at them and boss them around and rely on their tax dollars and treat them like an annoying housewife treats her husband. With market anarchy, there is no government to tell a man what to do, so the man has 100% total domination within the sphere of his own individual life, although he loses the fascist domination of men against women, because, absent government, no politics exists at all.

Left: Feminine: Individualist - Moderates and Independents, Liberals on the Center-Left: They want some freedom and so oppose total socialism, and they want some economic freedom, but they are deeply committed in principle to women's freedoms, abortion rights, LGBTQ rights, feminism, equality, and justice, and, in general, they want people to be nice and polite and respectful, and they take offense at the rude and offensive.

A "Non-Binary" is the name for someone who does not accept the gender binary or who does not fit within the gender binary or who adopts both masculine and feminine traits at the same time, or who is transgender and changes back and forth between being a man and being a woman. It is a term used often in the LGBTQ community, although I am the first author to assert that Non-Binary is the gender identity which is expressed in "political gender" as libertarian.

The Libertarian Non-Binary: economic freedom, which is freedom for men to be strong men, plus social freedom, which is freedom for women to be free women, free from oppression. Economic Right + Social Left.

The reason why Libertarianism always fails: Men on the Far Right, who embrace freedom and fall in love with the ideal of libertarian freedom, then realize that the principle of freedom would require freedom not only for men but also for women, as a matter of principle, and then they retreat, in fear of women, afraid of female freedom, and they return to fascism and social conservatism. And the men and women of the Center-Left, who become excited about freedom, that women can be truly free, later realize that the principle of freedom would also require freedom for men to be men, the freedom to be rude and offensive, the freedom to be strong, and so they become afraid of male freedom, and they retreat back to the Left, and have no place to go other than back to socialism. People are too afraid of true freedom because of their gender insecurity, because men can't stand seeing women be free, and women can't stand seeing men be free, so they retreat back into the gender safety of fascism for men and socialism for women.

The Libertarian hypothesis:

The condition of perfect male freedom is free market anarchy with zero government: a set of conditions where there is no government of men on behalf of women to boss around men and tell men what to do.

The condition of perfect female freedom is no oppression, which means, no laws that oppress women.

If there is no government, then there exists no government that can pass any laws, and, if there are no laws, then there are no laws that oppress women or violate women's rights. Under free market anarchy, men are free from government interference, and women are free from government oppression.

Therefore, the condition of perfect masculine freedom, and the condition of perfect feminine freedom, is the same set of conditions, which is equal to perfect freedom.

The anarcho-capitalist Far Right libertarians (known within the movement as the "An-Caps") have a principle, namely, Austrian economics. But the Non-Binary "Economic Right plus Social Left" libertarians, too, have a principle, although it is a different principle. The Non-Binary libertarian principle could be summed up as: "less government, more freedom." Let people do whatever they want.

In general, when the government stops telling people what to do, in economics, the result is behavior that the Right favors. People will trade in free markets, and be capitalists, unless the government forces them to pay taxes and obey regulations. But also, in general, when the government stops telling people what to do, in social policy, the result is behavior that is on the Left: absent government laws enforced by the police that ban the public from doing so, people will do drugs, people will use prostitutes, people will come in across borders from other countries, people will have gay weddings, people will have abortions, etc.

So, if you begin from the principle of "less government, more freedom," then you arrive at a place where your policy positions are economic Right plus social Left.

In general, social conservatives and the social Right are the ones who attack freedom in the social arena, while the economic Left are people who attack freedom in the economic sphere.

Therefore, to be a "social Left plus fiscal Right" Non-Binary libertarian (whom we could call by the abbreviation "NBL"), is to be opposed to both the social conservatives and fascists, and to oppose the economic Leftists and socialists, which means, to be opposed to government control and power as such, and to be a defender of liberty.

The economic Right is men being free. The social Right is men dominating women and preventing women from being free.

The social Left is women being free. The economic Left is men, on behalf of and for women, dominating men and preventing men from being free.

So a position that is economic Right plus social Left combines men being free and women being free.

This explains why the Non-Binary libertarian, the NBL, is on both the social Left and the economic Right.

In contrast, the true tyrant dictator would combine the social Right with the economic Left, much as the Nazis did, because the true tyrant desires to oppress and dominate both men and women, and allow neither one to have any degree of freedom.

In theory, along the lines of the gender of politics and the Libertarian as Non-Binary, there could also be a type of Libertarian, on the Left, who is a Libertarian only because they want freedom for women, and freedom for the weak and the oppressed, and they believe anarcho-capitalism is the best system suited to achieve this, and they do not care about men or freedom for men at all, men are not their area of concern. Such people do exist, although they seem to be rare and uncommon.

According to this theory of the gender of politics, a person who was neither on the Left nor on the Right, but who is unique, and is not on the political Left-Right binary at all, would also be a type of Non-Binary Libertarian, because they are not Left and not Right, they are not masc and they are not fem. However, we would expect each such type of person to have their own unique politics, so there would not be one name or word to describe their political identity.

Obviously, a state is the most common form of government, but, even in the condition of anarchy, even in a fully stateless society, I would define the initiation of violent force in order to achieve social, moral, or political goals, as a type of government, and as governing, even if the violence was used only by private individuals against other private individuals. This is why the Libertarian Party asks for a "loyalty oath," that a member will never initiate violence against a non-violent other to achieve social or political goals: because that oath really means you will not govern others. To the libertarian, violent force may be used only for individual self-defense, never to govern other people.

Libertarians often use a visual picture called The Nolan Chart, which is a diamond, with the Right on the right, the Left on the left, Freedom on the top, and Tyranny on the bottom. It is intended to show that Freedom would combine the economic side of the Right with the social side of the Left. It can be updated, using my analysis presented in this essay, merely be adding Masculine to the Right, Feminine to the Left, Collectivist to the bottom, and making the top Individualist.

Some concluding thoughts on these topics:

To be LGBTQ gay: to appreciate the beauty of strength.

To be a feminist: to appreciate the strength of beauty.

As with politics, where a side of Left or Right can have a gender, so, too, a race, as a political class, can also have a gender. We often see a vulnerable or oppressed race move to the Left when it is weak and chooses to be submissive in order to rely on the strength of the government to protect it, and then, once the race has its footing and is stable, the men of that race then move to the Right in order to assert their masculinity.

We saw this in America with the Jews, who used to be on the Left when they were weak but moved to the Right as they became strong, and, more recently, the Latinos have made the same move, the same dance step, they were politically weak and they had been on the Left, but the Latino men are moving to the Right today in order to assert their manhood and masculinity, against what they perceive as a weak, girly, womanly Left.

Interestingly, the men of the Black race seem not to do this; the Black people seem locked in a position of weakness and submitting to the state and relying upon the government for power on the Left side of politics. Black young men (and this is probably merely a false racial stereotype, or it may be true of some Black men but not be true of other Black men) tend to assert their manhood through violence, aggression, sex with women, drug use, gangs and gang-inspired music, daring feats of strength against the police and against authority, etc., instead of through Right-wing politics. There is also a certain type of white young man who copies the Black young man's criminal behaviors in order to assert his own white-young-man's masculinity, by doing drugs and having sex and breaking the law and such, although, being white, he is arrested for it far less frequently than the Black man.

The above is not intended to be racist towards the Black race. This is not intended to describe all Black men, but, instead, it describes a certain type of Black young man who is insecure in his masculinity, because these behaviors are done to assert one's manhood, and to overcome one's masculine insecurity. The math and logic of it is that, when a person breaks the law or defies authority, he is asserting that his negative N against the police and against the government is bigger than their negative N was against him, which is why he won his fight against them. And, when he has sex with a woman, he feels that his negative N was large enough to overcome her negative N against him, that he conquered her by having sex with her.

These behaviors are common in young men of every race, at the age where they are insecure in their masculinity, but, for whatever reason, media and culture tend to focus on this lifestyle among Black young men (and Latino young men, too). Possibly, because historically the Black race and the Latino race were oppressed and conquered by the white race for such a long time, and so they feel that they were dominated in the way that a man dominates a woman, some Black and Latino young men enter the world feeling that their masculinity has already been called into question, so they overcompensate by asserting their manhood in such cheap and easy ways as drugs and crime and gangs. It is all about the size of one's power to inflict negative N, the size of one's masculinity. Obviously there are entire classes of normal middle-class law-abiding Blacks and Latinos who are fully secure in their masculinity (or femininity) and to whom such would not apply, and these people tend to blend in with the moderates and independents of the white race, within the space between Right and Left.

It is also worth speculating that a certain type of political activist or politician feels masculine insecurity due to a history of racial or gender or class oppression against them, and then attacks people with their Leftism and attacks people with their socialism, against what they perceive as the complacent capitalist middle class or their foes on the political Right, in order to assert their negative energy against others to reclaim their lost manhood, by means of politics.

But we see in those rare cases when a Black man does achieve wealth and power, and when he no longer benefits from reliance upon the government for help, he too will move to the political Right in order to assert his masculinity, as, for example, with a very famous and notorious Black man United States Supreme Court Justice on the Right, Clarence Thomas, or else he will assume the white male position of privilege and power in the Left, as for example with America's recent Black President, Barack Obama, who had far more in common with rich white men on the Left than he did with the poor Black man on the streets.

In the United States of America, historically, the white race, in general, seems to be gender-male, and historically the white man had expected white women to submit to men. This explains the Right's fascination with the white race: it is because both of them are gender-masculine in their gender-performance. But people can be racist whether they are on the Right or on the Left. The white men on the Left tend to come to power on the Left, and to rise to the top of the Left, and they are the men who fight for women, they are the men who fight on behalf of those whom they deem weak, they are not themselves gendered as women, they wield negative N for women, not positive N as women. To hold power, and use helping those who are weak as your pretext and propaganda to rule, is certainly not the same thing as actually really being weak yourself. A rich man who donates millions of dollars to charity is not himself a beggar, and he has power and will never suffer as the beggar does; nor is a white man on the Left someone who truly is gender-feminine. He says he fights for them, but he is not them, he has no way to relate to them, it is a pretext to wield power over men on the justification of helping women.

Note here that I define "man" as someone who uses negative N as their survival strategy, and I define "woman" as someone who uses positive N as their survival strategy. I do not intend to refer to men and women by their bodies; here I speak of men and women as gender roles. In practice, sometimes, however, the body, the gender role, and the race, and the politics, will all blur together.

Also note that, while the caveman gender dynamic calls for a man to attack his woman's enemies with his causing –N to them, the man, to be as strong as possible, will fight everyone around him, in order to build toughness and strength, and, so, often the man will attack his woman herself with his –N also, just because she is nearby, even though protecting her in return for her +N to him was the basic premise of their social contract. Thus, man will attack woman's enemies, and man will attack woman at the same time, and this makes sense, from the man's point of view, as agent of –N.

This is why the Black woman leads the most challenging life: she is a woman, and so caveman gender roles define her as weak and submissive and for a man to dominate, and then she is also Black, so racial expressions of gender roles again treat her like the cavewoman gender role.

However, the solution for caveman gender is not for the Left to defeat the Right, as both Left and Right assume this caveman-cavewoman dynamic; the author feels that the Non-Binary Libertarian will emerge as the superior method of achieving gender freedom. The men in power on the Left do not truly desire gender equality, although the Leftist activists and radicals on the streets believe that they do; instead, the men want power, and they think they get more power if they wield it in the name of women and against men, by ruling the economy. But the Right is no better, because they only want freedom for men, and they desire to rule women, and so, despite their rhetoric of freedom, they are no friends of liberty. Only the Non-Binary Libertarians can achieve perfect freedom.

I will conclude this section with this thought, which is that, in perfect socialism, the people have only positive N, however, all their capacity for inflicting negative N is taken by the socialist government, and the government itself then inflicts negative N, on behalf of the people, against all critics and dissidents and rebels. This is why, much as the fascist men in power on the Right will censor or jail or shoot and murder their critics, political dissidents, and rebels, so, too, the socialist men in power on the Left would do the same thing, and cause incredible extreme negative N, despite the fact that their premise is everything being nice and pretty and beautiful and one big happy family of +N for everyone.

+N and –N are inherent in human existence, positive energy and negative energy is inherent in the very fabric of reality itself, in physics and chemistry, so +N and –N will never go away, the only question is which social and political institutions we choose to channel them into a form that we prefer, be they Left, Right, and/or Libertarian.

Insecurity in being a man: Fear that –N isn't big enough for Y –N to O. "I'm not strong enough."

Insecurity in being a woman: Fear that +N isn't big enough for Y +N to O. "I'm not good-looking enough."

Challenge to masculinity: Test of Y –N to O by means of O –N to Y.

Challenge to femininity: Test of Y +N to O by means of competitor or rival's +N to O.

Why adults tend to be more confident than young people: They have survived to adulthood, which proves, mathematically and logically, that the size of their N is big enough for them to survive.

Advertiser and politician manipulation: Subconsciously challenge masculinity or femininity (see above for how this is done), then sell a symbol of boost of Power = –N to men, or sell a symbol of boost of Beauty = +N to women. It doesn't have to be the real thing, what they sell is just a symbol of the thing.

END

ABOUT THE AUTHOR

Russell Hasan

Russell Hasan (pronouns: He, him, his) is a graduate of Vassar College, where his major was philosophy, and he graduated with Honors from the University of Connecticut School of Law, where he was an Editor of the Insurance Law Journal. He is a proud member of the LGBTQ community and an equally proud member of the Libertarian Party. Mr. Hasan has served as a member of the LGBTQ Rights Committee of the New York City Bar Association. He has been a volunteer program leader at the Triangle Community Center, which is the largest LGBTQ community center in southwestern Connecticut. He has also served as Vice Chair and Secretary of the Libertarian Party Affiliate of Fairfield County, Connecticut. He loves coffee and chewing gum, and he enjoys watching sports (Yankees baseball, Giants football, UConn Women's Basketball), comedies, and science fiction/fantasy tv shows and movies. His favorite novels are Atlas Shrugged, The Fountainhead, and Catch-22; his favorite tv show is Friends; and his favorite movies are Star Wars: The

Empire Strikes Back and The Matrix.

Mr. Hasan accepts fan mail and questions from readers at this email address:

author.russell.hasan@outlook.com

Bibliography:

Russell Hasan is the author of these books:

NONFICTION ESSAYS:

A System of Legal Logic: Using Aristotle, Ayn Rand, and Analytical Philosophy to Understand the Law, Interpret Cases, and Win in Litigation (A Scholarly Monograph)

Everything is Something: A Philosophical Dialogue About Logic, Language, Words, Meanings, Truth, and The Theory of Things

If P Then Q: Why Philosophy Can Teach You How to Think and Help You Live a Happy Life By the Methods of Applying Logic to Solve the Problems in Your Life and Achieve Success (A Scholarly Monograph)

Moral Logic and Economic Logic: On Knowledge, Choice, Will, Desire, The Moral Ideal, Economics, and Economic Value, with a System of Symbolic

Logical Notation

On Moral Psychology and Moral Philosophy: Towards a New Theory of Emotions, Motivations, and Ethics, Using the Insight that Emotions Pay Moral Debts and Moral Credits Owed to Self and Loved Ones (also published under the alternate first edition title: On Forgiveness)

The Power of Objectivism: Ayn Rand and John Galt and Atlas Shrugged and The Morality of Life, Intelligence, Greed, Selfishness, Rationality, Individuality, Integrity, Capitalism, Desire, and Freedom

What They Won't Tell You About Objectivism: Thoughts on the Objectivist Philosophy in the Post-Randian Era

Rand's Axiom Problem: On Objectivity, Ontology, Essence, Epistemology, Deduction, Induction, and the Foundations of Knowledge

An Essay on Reason and Perception

Golden Rule Libertarianism: A Defense of Freedom in Social, Economic, and Legal Policy

Libertarian Economics: A Manifesto and an Explanation

Economics: A Theory of Capital (also published under the alternate first edition title: XYAB Economics: A GOLD Libertarian Analysis of Money, Trade, and Freedom)

The Ethics and Morality of Human Sexuality

SELF-HELP:

To Be Loved, Love; To Be Liked, Be Nice to People; To Be an Adult, Forgive People: Emotions and Social Interactions, Explained

On Self-Reliance, Self-Esteem, and Intellectual Honesty

Love Without Labels: The Fifteen Questions and Answers that Define Your Gender Identity, Sexual Orientation, and Relationship Status

LAW:

A Law and Economics Approach to Litigation Costs: The Proportionality Test for E-Discovery Law (A Scholarly Monograph)

NONFICTION ANTHOLOGIES:

The Apple of Knowledge: Introducing the Philosophical Scientific Method and Pure Empirical Essential Reasoning

The Collected Essays on Logic of Philosopher Russell Hasan: The Complete System of Hasanian Logic, Presented in a Collection of Seven Essays

MEMOIR:

One Walked into the Spider's Web: A Gay Boy Goes to Vassar

FICTION:

The Paradise Machine: A Science Fiction Adventure Romance Novella, with The Slave Girl: A Fantasy Short Story (Russell's Paradise Found Book One)

The Magic Key Cards: A Science Fiction Thriller Suspense Spy Adventure Conspiracy Theory Comedy (Russell's Paradise Found Book Two)

Fallen Angel and Other Contemporary Coming-of-Age Romance Short Stories (Russell's Paradise Found Book Three)

The Throne War - A Sword & Sorcery LitRPG Dark Fantasy with a Boy Thief, a Knight, a Ninja, a Sorceress, Monsters, an Evil King, and Lots of RPG-Style Combat (The Golden Wand Trilogy Book One)

The Shadow of Heaven - A Sword & Sorcery LitRPG Dark Fantasy with Heroes, Elves, Dragons, Vampires, a Quest, and Lots of RPG-Style Combat (The Golden Wand Trilogy Book Two)

The Castle in the Sky - A Sword & Sorcery LitRPG Dark Fantasy with Gods, a War, and an RPG-Combat-Style Final Battle Between Good and Evil (The Golden Wand Trilogy Book Three)

The Golden Wand Trilogy (omnibus boxed-set edition)

Project Utopia: A Libertarian Science Fiction Anthology

The Office of Heavenly Restitution: A Fantasy Fiction Anthology

The Prince, The Girl and The Revolution: A Science Fiction Fairy Tale

Rob Seablue and The Eye of Tantalus

GAMES:

WARM HAPPY FRIENDLY Core Rulebook, First Edition: The Guessing Game and Trading Game of Supply and Demand

www.ingramcontent.com/pod-product-compliance
Lightning Source LLC
Chambersburg PA
CBHW070054260726

48658CB00002B/878